say, a river

Pam Schindler

say, a river

Acknowledgements

I am grateful to the late Drue Heinz and the Hawthornden Foundation for a writer's fellowship at Hawthornden Castle, Lasswade, Scotland, in 2013, where some of these poems were written.

Warm thanks to my Brisbane poets' group, for years of sharing new work and friendship in poetry. I am also grateful to Zenobia Frost, Jeffrey Harpeng, Ron Heard, Anne Kellas and Ynes Sanz for thoughtful reading of the manuscript.

My appreciation to photographer Mila Zincone for permission to use the cover image.

say, a river
ISBN 978 1 76109 496 5
Copyright © text Pam Schindler 2023
Cover image: *Melaleucas* © Mila Zincone 2018

First published 2023 by
GINNINDERRA PRESS
PO Box 3461 Port Adelaide 5015
www.ginninderrapress.com.au

Contents

Flame-tree

Flame-tree	9
Rain	10
Half a moon	11
Man sleeping	12
Landscape	13
The leaving	14
say, a river	15
Or this way	16
The launch	17
The easterly spell	18
Like a river	19
The old track signs: Little Lake Valley	20
Littoral	21
At Lake Weyba	22
From the old orchard	23
The Bosc pears	24
that which	25

Like someone who is leaving

After the fires, Kinglake (2)	29
Like someone who is leaving	30
Silver dollar	31
Nets	32
In September, the river	33
The birds at her window	34
The last miles	36
First day after	37
Morning with pardalotes	38
Three boats	39

The keeping of your heart	40
North Esk River, April	43
Drummond of Hawthornden	44
The old track signs: Lake Holmes	45
White flag irises	47
grasshopper	48

My mother's spade

Stargazing for the blind: an app	51
My mother's spade	52
Cat in a storm	53
If they came	54
At Assisi	55
Perfect pitch	56
The grass	57
Pandani walking	58
Night on the island	59
Painting the Noosa	60
Morning after	61
The pandemic considered as a cyclone	62
Stolpersteine (stumbling stones)	63
Windy at Iona	64
To Loch Ossian	65
Cumquats, Hobart	66
As if, curlews	67
fig-tree/fig-bird	68
Scribbly	69

Publications	70
Awards	70

Flame-tree

Flame-tree

the flame-tree scatters
little silk goblets, Chinese-red
loosed handfuls of scarlet

the storm, passing at a distance,
is a clot of dark gestures,
flung brushstrokes – stilled,
suspended

and the flame-tree scatters
the light red and the dark red
little stemmed cups

and it is a tree scattering itself
against the light
mingling red into its own shade

exclaiming itself
in wet red silk
against the painted light

Rain

I went out
in the slow bloom of rain,
wet petals on my skin

the sleeping ibis
were folded white packages
lodged in the high branches

I went out into the white air,
into the misty quiet

the river slipping fast,
striped darkness and silver

I swam under a cataract
of hectic lorikeet chatter

then out into the calm, the eddy
the slow warm bloom

in the riverbank trees
the slow warm bloom of rain

Half a moon

Come and stay,
there'll be half a moon by Sunday,
a gleaming bowlful of dark

enough to feed
the lover in me, the elusive
heart in you –
all the lost chances,

they are here still,
turning in sleep
in the dark bowl
the new moon comes carrying
like a gift.

Man sleeping

it curls beside me at night
flanks just touching
it is sunk deep in sleep

it is a man, or
rather it is an ocean
sleeping along the sand

under its reflective sky
the tribes who breathe water
are finning their unseen trails –

rapt, under the moon,
their marvellous seasons
of seeding and rebirth –

I would draw your hips to me
their silvery catch
but you have gone deep

far under the swell and sparkle,
with the slow breath of waves
and you would not know me there

Landscape

after Dorothy Napangardi's *Karntakurlangu Jukurrpa*

I remember arriving with the grasstree spikes
in creamy flower, taller than a man,
the birds balancing to feed
on such cones of sweetness
in the excited air –

the dead in their trees, speaking and sighing,
the wind in their leaves –

the locked and breaking
honeycomb of days

the hooked blanket of the land
the mesh of light
the tongues of the white rain

The leaving

For Anne

your brother with you as you walk
down to where the air goes fuzzy with salt
and a boat carves the green bay,
a cormorant on every channel-marker

you sing him a hymn from childhood
the sand braided with the tide
jellyfish like heavy-petalled glass flowers
sea eagles rafting the wind

too late to touch him,
and too far – but you sing
of childhood and the small waves of the bay,
and walk with him until

it is suddenly too deep
and he goes on without you

say, a river

say, a river of dark honey
say cormorant, a swimming
neck and head

curved the wet black neck
diving through, flecked with gold
the sliding dark
river dusted with leaves, with sun
dusted with glint, touched
with the tip of the brush – say
goanna, its tail on the ridged bark
finely dotted with yellow, scales of
paint on the slow curve bending
the honey river, its dark flank
speckled with light, with dust
spreading wide under the shine
of sharp leaves brittle
banksia and she-oak
soft-flaking paperbark
river of slow honey, say dark
river of light

Or this way

On 'Probably' by Anne Kellas

not that way, Anne
not for me
the fearful plunge
into the heaving dark

I will head out across the shallows
the flat shelving seabed
ankle-deep, dappled with sun

and flatten myself like a stingray
into a resting hollow
and pull up the sand like a sheet

and lie invisible
under the fine white sand
while the sunstruck sea
sighs and breathes above me

The launch

on a painting by Charles Blackman

they have laid her to sleep
in a bank of flowers

she is curled, eyes closed
into a dream of earth

the child, the bride
they have launched her like a boat

like a boat she has slipped
into a swoon of sky

lit by white petals –
and founders, willingly

into the caress of dark blooms
into the knowing tide

The easterly spell

Blackmans Bay, Tasmania

the bay was pewter, the sky
the bloom on a blue plum

and now, in the wind off the sea,
rain is feathering down like snow

the boat moored inside the headland
is a drag of dark paint in the surging grey

each leaf of the spinning gum
is a silver owl's face

and at nightfall we almost disappear –
quiet settling among the houses

the moon breathing silver
the rain weaving the air

Like a river

I will carry you
like a river full of rain

its silver weave
slubbed with darkness
where the current catches

we will turn
like a sleeper turning,
into the pull of dark

the light on your back like silk –
we will slide down together
on that tide

skin remembers skin
and even the moon's hands
catch on your silky back

warm answers to warm
and I remember you
like a river remembering the rain

The old track signs: Little Lake Valley

Overland Track, Tasmania
i.m. O. Vaughan

Not many words here,
the wind blows them away.
See how the lichen has crept and flowered
into the cuts that make the letters –
'Little Lake Valley', a lilt
unheard until the words are spoken,
voiced on the high air, where the valley
drops away below.
To the birds and the seasons,
the ice and the waking frogs,
the dark and the brilliant light,
this is not a lonely place.
Let me cut such words on the clear air.
Little Lake Valley is where I will leave your name.

Littoral

days of wind and glitter –
in the swampy hollow

unseen spiders have strung
bowls of white sunlight in the reeds

white that blurs upward like smoke
from driftnets of sun –

they have floated circles of fire
among the grey-green stems –

bird and cicada
reed and trill and rasp

the lake opens like an eye
of liquid dark

fiddler crabs back away up the bank,
raise a mahogany claw –

country that soars and flickers
red mud and brilliant sand

its flag is the brahminy kite

and the breathing mangrove feet
that wait for the sigh of the tide

At Lake Weyba

for Beth Crawter

she-oaks with sun in their hair
lean and shine and whisper

the friarbird's acid twang
loops the tea-tree like a vine

Beth's house is in paperbark country
under the lake's spell

frogs bongo and chatter
stars like sandgrit, a mopoke moon

the old dog dreaming on the veranda
gathers it all into his sleep

just as the lake does, holding
cloud and chatter and blue,

the day's light and lilt, all
awash among the mangrove roots

From the old orchard

For Norelle Lickiss

these are old apples
more fat than tall
in firm squat wheels,
in green skin,
red-feathered
where the sun wells up

grubs mine them
leaving dry wounds,
dark as figs
eat them with a knife!
you said

in company
they turn the fruit bowl thoughtful
resting, as their last leaves
curl and brown

outliving, for a while
the season that made them
floating, streaked with summer
tumbled hip to hip

The Bosc pears

in this season the pears –
slender, long-waisted
cinnamon odalisques
with weighty hips –

arrive, golden in the leaf-light

once picked, they put on
a ceramic calm
stilled, like a vase,
like a cat,
a hidden ripeness
under a roughened glaze

tipped on one side
they fall into curves,
their hips invite –
'reclining nude' –
their Modigliani calm
their Matisse effulgence

that which

like the sliding river
like the tree whose hair
slips in a whim of breeze

cannot be claimed
can be listened for
can crouch in a pause
can be lapsed into

can murmur, under the river's skin
can be remembered

Like someone who is leaving

After the fires, Kinglake (2)

for Sue Gunningham

she is keeping the bricked veranda
she sweeps it clear of leaves
these grey stains
are where the windowglass melted
onto the bricks
she is keeping it clear of leaves

Nature is cheerful here
the trees thronging back
head-high already
after less than two years
bright leaves dress the black trunks
and the small creek is singing its stones again

it is all that is left of the house

she unfolds a chair on the bricks
above the valley hazed with burnt trees
and the air resounds
with his heartbeat, his loss

she is sweeping the brick veranda
she is keeping it clear of leaves

Like someone who is leaving

this morning I catch myself putting things away
like someone who is leaving
like someone who will never use dishes again

a thousand miles to the south, your sons
feel for the slot behind the rose bushes,
let themselves in with the spare key,
find the shoes, side by side,
the half-worn shirts, soft with your shape,
the sheets quiet on your bed, all
forgetful now

that for a while they clothed
your kindling smile
and those thin hands I loved

and I have slipped back too
from dishes and work and shoes
to follow you a little way

as far as yearning will take me
toward wherever you have gone

Silver dollar

in my father's pocket
a silver dollar,
rubbed to a blurry moon

the moon is worn down
like the saint's bronze hand
with so much touching and wishing –
she is polished to a shine

– coin in the pocket,
jingled and rubbed –
and she is so much softer,
silver to his bronze

that I search her skin
for the prints of your fingers
that turned and turned
your lucky dollar, your wishing moon

that slipped free, finally, sailing high
over your unfinished years

Nets

For Emerald Roe

I am here on a silver coast
where the sky pools
in abalone shells

a bowl of sea
bounded by blue
mountains and islands

and the hungry gull's cry

I am here to watch
while a few days
open and shut like clams
pause and turn and run out
like the tide

to string my paper net
for the tide to run through

here on the chill sand
to wade through threaded light

to gather morning sticks
for the flames to run through

In September, the river

catching under the city's din
the river's old yearning

how each afternoon
the wind comes to us with brown arms
with bare sandy feet

the old lull and sway
is back in the spring air
remember, remember
the lilt of the moving river
its colours of mud and sky

(I weary of work, I forget the point
of shopping malls)

meanwhile the river's salty hair
streams to the bay islands
where mangroves grow on a line
inked under sky-glitter

take me back
to the knife and cup
the silvered boards and tin
that cast a square of shade
under the salt wind

The birds at her window

i.

at her veranda the palms gather,
trees feathered like birds –

but the palms never come to the window,
folding their wings, looking
for something to eat, she says

and when the round moon rises
and the palms shift their fronds
in a breeze of silver light,

it doesn't make any sound, she says
we don't hear the moon calling

ii.

I bring her the fallen
frangipani flowers

their curved, white wings

five pure petals cupping
a well of sun

they're *perfect,* she says
– and *silent*

iii.

there are birds here,
or their gestures,
their daubed lorikeet colours –

in these days, a tree
might voice its heart's call,
palms might arrive at the window
to feed and preen

we watch storm clouds at sunset,
their gilded towers
dimming into blue –
when it's getting ready to say goodbye,
it's like a flower opening, she says

and rain sweeps the roof,
and the moon visits again –

she is listening
for the moon's pure carolling,
the breeze and sweep of its wings

The last miles

how long does this go on, she asked me,
how many hundreds of miles?

all the way to the sea, I said,
where the road
ends in a patch of sand,

the foam rushes around your feet
and the waves
shine and break in the sun –

so slow these miles, where she lies
and struggles, like a broken bird –

may she skim the last stretch, arriving
to the slant of seabirds crying
another day, another heart
to their salt, tumultuous home

where the world breaks on the sand,
and all day the sea
forgets, and forgets
and remembers

First day after

I brought you with me
that first morning –
you borrowed my face
to feel the sun

around us the butcherbird voices
in strained clarity
sang the heart of the day –
you were listening too

I counted first things
as they arrived without you –
I brought you a cloud, a bird
a slant of light,
offered them one by one

and then you gave them back:

the first moon, golden,
that you brought me with both arms

Morning with pardalotes

the wind has wakened in the night
pouring from the mountains and the dark ocean
and birds tinier than thought
birds of glance or whim
with a three-note cry
flit on the wild air

the grass is silvered with seed
blown and flung with wind –
a rough spirit in sudden possession –
where the wallabies came to feed at dusk,
grey, in the sculptured stillness,
see! the grass, beaten with light

on this island we are closer to the turning sky,
spinning into our own weather,
far from the lull of the tropics –
birds on the wind, almost invisible, gathering
glimpse and syllable, lifted
like pardalotes, jottings, flown –

Three boats

Blackmans Bay, Tasmania

Inside the south headland
two small yachts and a catamaran
stay moored for months,

their faded red and blue
painted with the changing light
as they turn to face the wind;

each with its mast and staylines
like Charlotte's spider daughters
the three who stayed behind

sketching their simple webs
in the plain barn window –
a frame for all their days

'We like this place, and we like you'
when the others had sailed away.

The keeping of your heart

1 Bluebells

I came to the Esk when the valley woke
stretching stiff fingers
new green unfolding in the cold
the cliff a reddish haze of buds.

I followed the small, swift river
to the slope above the gorge
where bluebells grow. Too early,
just buds, swollen at the base of the leaves.
Wind tossed light among the green blades.
Small birds called over a wave
of imminent blue.

I would wake you with this spring.
I would wake you like a bird,
calling over fields of blue.

2 The magpie, balancing

the magpie, balancing
high in a hoop-pine,
surveying the morning
carries his dead lightly
in wing and bone

upturned dinghies rain-slicked,
the island hills painted out with cloud

but how shall we carry you,
now that you have gone where
cameras cannot hold you,
telephones cannot find your voice?

gulls and oystercatchers pace the beach,
the slick edge light-painted

another morning opens
on a day that you cannot count

we will bring
for currency, shells in our pockets
for password, the tui's husky music

how shall we carry you?
bare feet stepping onto the sand –

a thin moon cradling the dark
and a magpie balancing

3 The ginger fox

a ginger fox looked back at me
for a long moment
then loped away up the track

and I have a part
in the keeping of your heart

there was snow on the wind
yet the sun glittered

and this is part
of the keeping of your heart

the trees broke into leaves soft as petals
and the bluebells waited in their pale buds

ah, blown galaxy of leaves!
I will gather them all
for the keeping of your heart

North Esk River, April

A fine dust of rain fell out of the sun,
the path was moss and mud,
and the day's great wheel carried us
and all the trees with their thousand budding fingers
through the cold air of spring –

A green field glowed through the grey branches.
It's quite a spiritual walk, said the man with two dogs,
surprising me with the word,
and the birds small as leaves
and the sudden hail sharp around our ears
sang, and flew, and glittered.

Drummond of Hawthornden

who built this house
to frame and invite
a piece of countryside?

spring wells in the trees'
fine fingers, hazing the cliff-side

the grey bushes wear
a tinsel of small bird calls

this house invites the rushing river
the small bats wheeling suddenly
into view at dusk

its windows cherish
the far bank of the gorge,
pointillist, each brushmark
quickening with spring

what matter if he also romanticised,
gilding its 'classic shades'?

this valley breaks sweetly into spring,
the house honouring its ancient heart

The old track signs: Lake Holmes

Overland Track, Tasmania

Lake Holmes, this one says,
with three nails marching down
through the middle of each word
   LA:KE
HOL.MES
each letter edged
with a small fog of weathering,
of frayed silver wood –
two English words posted
to stand watch here,
by this tannin-dark lake
through the wind and snow,
the brilliant light –
since someone decided that Holmes
was worthy of a lake.

Lichen has flowered
over the crossbeam of the H
while the S, angular, jerks
through thirty years of growth rings,
the chisel awkward at the curves;
and here it hints
at the hands we cannot know
the ranger who cut it
some flickering evening
from a board of mountain pine

but to know its old name
is beyond our listening

and before that? a presence
of darkness and silver, nameless
dip in the moraine,
a pool for the wind's shaping.

White flag irises

I am planting white flag irises,
the kind you cut
from the hundreds blowing at dusk
in a stony field,
and brought them, wet and fragile
into the lighted kitchen,
and piled them in my arms –

Tipped into the palm,
they hardly seem to be seeds,
these dual paper discs
the size of an 'o'
with a seed pasted inside,
a dot of memory –
your hands gathering the blooms,
yellow-white among the lichened stones –

and not meant for keeping,
meant to scatter in the wind.

grasshopper

thin as a needle, living,
blown through with light, the glass-
green of new leaves, tensed,
he bows to left and right
on filaments of knees
jumps! from my sleeve's
inedible leaf
into the dark the looming
crescent of the world

My mother's spade

Stargazing for the blind: an app

For Yuma Decaux and Jake Dean, Brisbane engineering students who in 2018 created an app to enable virtual stargazing for people with low vision/blindness.

blind under the night sky
he ponders how to map
the pull of unseen presences

how stars and their distances
could be bird calls in a forest,
measurable points of sound

most stars are imagined anyway
(he points the phone with its app
at Orion under our feet)

already we hold them in place
with something other than sight

astronomy is an imaginary art
its vast archipelagos
invisible as mathematics

he conjures its shining islands
tagging them with sound
feeling them branch out around him

till the wayward gods
who have seen his type before
send him a silent smile

My mother's spade

after the heat of the day
a storm floated up the sky
in bruise-coloured waves

and blessed my plantings,
basil and parsley, renewing
the garden patch

dug with my mother's spade
wood-handled and sturdy,
only a little rusty

bringing flashings and collisions
and fingernails of rain on the roof

welcome! in the bones of my hands,
welcome, mother of mine –

from across the backyards a trumpet
played bright, celebratory scales

Cat in a storm

For Ron Heard

When the thunder began gathering
its boulders together
and hail struck at the roof
with metal claws,
the cat crouched
in her safest place –
a small centre of self-possession –
a cat under a car under a house—

while the sky gnashed
and the wind heaved
the great wings of the palms,
she, who is quicksilver,
became pebble, became snail,
drawing her four feet
into the safety of a circle,
and slept in the curl of the storm.

If they came

If they came to find me,
I could hide in a hollow tree
and cast no shadow.
They would see only the tree trunks.

Like a pippie between waves
I could tip myself on end
and tunnel down into the wet sand.
They would see only the curving beach.

I could chisel a cave in the cliff
and lie safe when hail
swept the valley. And if they came,
they would see only the stone ridge.

But now, old as I am,
it's time to cast a shadow.

Stone, wave and tree
will eat me soon enough.

At Assisi

our tents are tucked into the hills' shoulder
deep in leaves and fallen chestnuts
wind sweeps the haze from the valley
sharpens the stars over Assisi

how you lit up our meeting
worth turning aside
from all my known ways
for another such talk

marking an invisible waystation
you have tied two sticks
in a pilgrim's cross outside your tent

today you climbed high over Assisi
to talk to the shepherds
then came striding down, just before dark,
vivid in the cold air

are you a pilgrim, then?

this place makes me a pilgrim,
you said

Perfect pitch

'e' is yellow as a pear
'd' and 'g' are warm and woody
'f' is bright citrus

each key has its palette of notes
the flats are stained glass
the sharps all striving

like 'a', your key, a heart
strung on its three sharps
its candid white notes

fingers were the way in
to that place of liquid light

it waited always, a sudden
corner to be turned

in scales my fingers recited its colours
they cascaded in like water

your voice – not so much the pitch
as the colour of it – unmistakeable,

that first day when I had to cross my arms
so as not to seize
at once all the gold of you

they say perfect pitch wanes with age

if another such certainty comes my way
may I know it like any bird

and follow it

The grass

in Cooma every day
a man goes out with pencil and paper
to draw the grass

clouds boil up from the ocean
the mountains fling them high
they skate out over the Monaro's
dry granite hills
glitter of gum and wattle
suspended, turbulent –

a man goes out to draw
the wind, the turning days
the grasses carrying light like a wave

a man goes out to draw
the light that pours through a grass blade

a man goes out to the grass

with a pencil
he slows the sun

Pandani walking

maybe the pandani walk at night
flexing their long pale toes
bracing when the salt wind
rattles their paper hair

now they stoop, darkening the shade
around a cottage
now they wade stiffly
the white waves' edge

they lope, their pineapple fruit
splits into glossy molars
golden on the midnight grass

toothless again, they stand thoughtful
heads touching, a deep shade

who sleeps at their bony ankles
for shelter in sun or rain?

a breath is warm in their branches,
a stray hand
plaits their leaves with stars

Night on the island

night is a slatted path through the white sand,
cool and smooth underfoot

shut down sight, and
the island is built of frog calls, cross-hatched,
an eager sawing

my torch catches rhinestones on the path
the eyes of glass spiders

unseen in the dunes the curlews
croon over their eerie children

the stars crowd the sky with white –
below, banksias raise a shadow-heaven,
clotted with black cones

I leave two walls of the tent open,
and wake to find the breeze moving over my bare back
and the surf thundering

Painting the Noosa

Noosa River, Queensland

I daub-in the tumbling sea roar,
distance-dimmed,
and on that ground
I stub the crow-notes, crooned, effortful,
dark paint squirted from the tube.
Then a cross-hatching of small voices,
the whip-bird's sailing line
of fluent yellow,
blue reeds crowding the river's edge
in a haze of pencilled whispers.

A glint of anklebones
under the reddish lilt – then my feet
set off the crinkling murmur
of a body in water, breaking across,
rocking the reflected trees – I skew,
I tilt the whole canvas, to the waiting
embrace of the river, almost-heard
bass notes of sky and treacle, the river's
sprawled golden body, its dark eye
winking up from silent depths.

Morning after

I wash the soup bowls
sticky with pumpkin,
rinse out the glasses.
I set the coffee pot quiet on the shelf.

The old griefs are quieter too
in the morning sun –
your heart, after so much raging,
almost cool to touch.

I dare not look at you
but I watch your hands
set ripe tomatoes in a green bowl,
calmly, though the colours shiver.

The pandemic considered as a cyclone

From our island, the virus was like a cyclone
gyring unseen off our coasts –
blooming on our screens,
on the weather radar,
in garish reds and yellows –

and like a cyclone, the invisible
cords of its strength,
that reach across continents,
pulled awry all the currents of the world
and brought us fear and confusion.

Stolpersteine (stumbling stones)*

A step and a stumble,
among the cobbles.
So that your foot will catch
and your voice will try
the name that went with a life,
the feet in shoes like yours.
On this street.
So that your voice would catch,
and your shoe.
To trip over a Jew.
A lazy curse,
for a stumbling stone –
stolper, the clumsy halting
perfect in the word.
Unbalanced, for a breath,
by this stone in your way,
this name under your feet.
In the shine of the rain,
the chill we would not linger in.
To speak their names.

* The Stolpersteine Project installs memorial plaques in the pavement to mark the places where individual victims of the Nazis last lived and worked freely.

Windy at Iona

the bay was scoured silver, pulsing with wind
sun flicked light out of a thousand grassblades
the sheep sheltered behind rocky outcrops
and the birds found clear green shallows
where a bluff was a broad back,
calming the north wind

clumps of black seaweed
crawled over the beach like spiders,
gusts travelled over the water
in rushes of glitter

and twelve Irish souls
rowed ashore in a black curragh
bright-faced,
sea-swept and cold

to this green island,
a foothold for the mighty sky

To Loch Ossian

Loch Ossian, Scotland

I walked
to Loch Ossian to listen
for the grey
words of the small
pyramidal rocks
islanded in silver

tor and *pebble* and *stone*
are the words we made
as we tried to catch
the whisper of the rocks,
unmoving, seeming to move
in the waves that shone
on Loch Ossian

sand and *boulder* and *scree,*
copying the sounds
we could almost hear –
insistent, saying what?
these small squat syllables,
adamant, in the lilting light,
in the shining wash

Cumquats, Hobart

These little orange globes –
lanterns that floated
in the tree at dusk –
have melted and spilled
their liquid weight,
bubbling into the dark sugar.

And I catch them in glass,
I slow them in their orange moment.

From the sun's golden roil,
they cool in a trance of calm.
In the dusk of the year,
at the far ebb of the sun.

As if, curlews

as if the turning world
drew birds to itself
now here, now here

the tilt of the days
calling them north, they lift
from the mild subtropics

their bodies wasting as they fly
from Queensland to Siberia
beating over the sea

the skies of half a world
drawn on their wings
till they land, spent, in the wakening

the hectic Arctic spring
thrumming around them, marshlands
thawing to the glint

and trickle of water, after
the long snow silence
the insect burgeoning

as if only such plenty
could feed such flight

fig-tree/fig-bird

the fig tree has a familiar

its dark-green leaves
drawn into a wing
its reddish fruit
ringing an eye

as if it grew birds from its branches,
birds of its kin and hue,
the thick leaf-clusters
lifting into flight

or as if the self
that inhabits this weighty tree
also flew and sang –
fig-birds, we say

naming a mystery

in its dark foliage
wings speak to leaves,
to hands – who is it
sings in this tree?

I think I am the sand's familiar
how it shapes feet for walking
for printing its skin

Scribbly

once, a mist of native bees
and once, parrot faces
at an open hollow

always the itch
of grubs in its painted bark,
tunnelled script in its skin

and always the sun-dapple,
body of sky, of leaves blown
in the breeze off the bay

it lifts great arms
to the slow drift of the days –
in the wear of so many seasons,
written and rewritten

body as shelter
body as branching dream
it is painted and storied
a trunk built of days

old man, he is busy
bees in his fingers
wind in his leaves
days sweet in his arms

Publications

I would like to thank the editors of the following magazines and anthologies where some of these poems have appeared:

Australian Poetry Journal, blue giraffe, Communion Arts Journal, Etchings, foam:e, Hecate, Island, Meanjin, the mozzie, Prospect, neither/nor, Scope, small packages, StylusLit, Verity La.

Australian Poetry Members' Anthologies 2012, 2014, 2015 and *2021.* Melbourne: Australian Poetry Ltd.

Yesterday's tomorrow: Words of COVID. (Brisbane): *The Creative Issue*, 2021.

Outer space, inner minds. Carindale, Queensland: Interactive Publications, 2020.

Grieve: stories and poems about grief and loss. Volume 7. The Junction, NSW: Hunter Writers Centre, 2019.

The sky falls down: an anthology of loss. Gina Mercer and Terry Whitebeach (eds). Port Adelaide, South Australia: Ginninderra Press, 2019.

Awards

'Landscape' was Highly Commended in the Philip Bacon Ekphrasis Award, Queensland Poetry Festival, 2016.

'The Leaving' was Commended in the W.B. Yeats Poetry Prize (Australia), 2019.

www.ingramcontent.com/pod-product-compliance
Lightning Source LLC
Chambersburg PA
CBHW072106110526
44590CB00018B/3337